AIRLINE PASSENGER FLIGHT LOG BOOK

THIS BOOK BELONGS TO:

NAME: _____

ADDRESS: _____

CITY: _____ STATE: _____

COUNTRY: _____ POSTAL/ZIP CODE: _____

PHONE: _____ EMAIL: _____

IF FOUND PLEASE CONTACT THE OWNER.

Cadmus Collection

DESTINATION:

DATE	AIRLINE	FLT. NO	AIRCRAFT TYPE	REGISTRATION	FROM	TO

JOURNAL

YEAR:

FLYING TIME	DISTANCE	REMARKS

Carried Forward

Grand Total

Total Number of Flights _____

DESTINATION:

DATE	AIRLINE	FLT. NO	AIRCRAFT TYPE	REGISTRATION	FROM	TO

JOURNAL

YEAR:

FLYING TIME	DISTANCE	REMARKS

		Carried Forward
		Grand Total

Total Number of Flights _____

DESTINATION:

DATE	AIRLINE	FLT. NO	AIRCRAFT TYPE	REGISTRATION	FROM	TO

JOURNAL

YEAR:

FLYING TIME	DISTANCE	REMARKS

		Carried Forward
		Grand Total

Total Number of Flights _____

DESTINATION:

DATE	AIRLINE	FLT. NO	AIRCRAFT TYPE	REGISTRATION	FROM	TO

JOURNAL

FLYING TIME	DISTANCE	REMARKS

		Carried Forward
		Grand Total

Total Number of Flights _____

DESTINATION:

DATE	AIRLINE	FLT. NO	AIRCRAFT TYPE	REGISTRATION	FROM	TO

JOURNAL

YEAR:

FLYING TIME	DISTANCE	REMARKS

Carried Forward

Grand Total

Total Number of Flights _____

DESTINATION:

DATE	AIRLINE	FLT. NO	AIRCRAFT TYPE	REGISTRATION	FROM	TO

JOURNAL

YEAR:

FLYING TIME	DISTANCE	REMARKS

Carried Forward

Grand Total

Total Number of Flights _____

DESTINATION:

DATE	AIRLINE	FLT. NO	AIRCRAFT TYPE	REGISTRATION	FROM	TO

JOURNAL

YEAR:

FLYING TIME	DISTANCE	REMARKS

		Carried Forward
		Grand Total

Total Number of Flights _____

DESTINATION:

DATE	AIRLINE	FLT. NO	AIRCRAFT TYPE	REGISTRATION	FROM	TO

JOURNAL

YEAR:

FLYING TIME	DISTANCE	REMARKS

Carried Forward

Grand Total

Total Number of Flights _____

DESTINATION:

DATE	AIRLINE	FLT. NO	AIRCRAFT TYPE	REGISTRATION	FROM	TO

JOURNAL

YEAR:

FLYING TIME	DISTANCE	REMARKS

		Carried Forward
		Grand Total

Total Number of Flights _____

DESTINATION:

DATE	AIRLINE	FLT. NO	AIRCRAFT TYPE	REGISTRATION	FROM	TO

JOURNAL

YEAR:

FLYING TIME	DISTANCE	REMARKS

		Carried Forward
		Grand Total

Total Number of Flights _____

DESTINATION:

DATE	AIRLINE	FLT. NO	AIRCRAFT TYPE	REGISTRATION	FROM	TO

JOURNAL

YEAR:

FLYING TIME	DISTANCE	REMARKS

Carried Forward

Grand Total

Total Number of Flights _____

DESTINATION:

DATE	AIRLINE	FLT. NO	AIRCRAFT TYPE	REGISTRATION	FROM	TO

JOURNAL

YEAR:

FLYING TIME	DISTANCE	REMARKS

		Carried Forward
		Grand Total

Total Number of Flights _____

DESTINATION:

DATE	AIRLINE	FLT. NO	AIRCRAFT TYPE	REGISTRATION	FROM	TO

JOURNAL

YEAR:

FLYING TIME	DISTANCE	REMARKS

Carried Forward

Grand Total

Total Number of Flights _____

DESTINATION:

DATE	AIRLINE	FLT. NO	AIRCRAFT TYPE	REGISTRATION	FROM	TO

JOURNAL

YEAR:

FLYING TIME	DISTANCE	REMARKS

Carried Forward

Grand Total

Total Number of Flights _____

DESTINATION:

DATE	AIRLINE	FLT. NO	AIRCRAFT TYPE	REGISTRATION	FROM	TO

JOURNAL

YEAR:

FLYING TIME	DISTANCE	REMARKS

		Carried Forward
		Grand Total

Total Number of Flights _____

DESTINATION:

DATE	AIRLINE	FLT. NO	AIRCRAFT TYPE	REGISTRATION	FROM	TO

JOURNAL

YEAR:

FLYING TIME	DISTANCE	REMARKS

Carried Forward

Grand Total

Total Number of Flights _____

DESTINATION:

DATE	AIRLINE	FLT. NO	AIRCRAFT TYPE	REGISTRATION	FROM	TO

JOURNAL

YEAR:

FLYING TIME	DISTANCE	REMARKS

		Carried Forward
		Grand Total

Total Number of Flights _____

DESTINATION:

DATE	AIRLINE	FLT. NO	AIRCRAFT TYPE	REGISTRATION	FROM	TO

JOURNAL

YEAR:

FLYING TIME	DISTANCE	REMARKS

		Carried Forward
		Grand Total

Total Number of Flights _____

DESTINATION:

DATE	AIRLINE	FLT. NO	AIRCRAFT TYPE	REGISTRATION	FROM	TO

JOURNAL

YEAR:

FLYING TIME	DISTANCE	REMARKS

Carried Forward

Grand Total

Total Number of Flights _____

DESTINATION:

DATE	AIRLINE	FLT. NO	AIRCRAFT TYPE	REGISTRATION	FROM	TO

JOURNAL

YEAR:

FLYING TIME	DISTANCE	REMARKS

Carried Forward

Grand Total

Total Number of Flights _____

DATE	AIRLINE	FLT. NO	AIRCRAFT TYPE	REGISTRATION	FROM	TO

JOURNAL

YEAR:

FLYING TIME	DISTANCE	REMARKS

Carried Forward

Grand Total

Total Number of Flights _____

DESTINATION:

DATE	AIRLINE	FLT. NO	AIRCRAFT TYPE	REGISTRATION	FROM	TO

JOURNAL

YEAR:

FLYING TIME	DISTANCE	REMARKS

Carried Forward

Grand Total

Total Number of Flights _____

DESTINATION:

DATE	AIRLINE	FLT. NO	AIRCRAFT TYPE	REGISTRATION	FROM	TO

JOURNAL

YEAR:

FLYING TIME	DISTANCE	REMARKS

		Carried Forward
		Grand Total

Total Number of Flights _____

DESTINATION:

DATE	AIRLINE	FLT. NO	AIRCRAFT TYPE	REGISTRATION	FROM	TO

JOURNAL

YEAR:

FLYING TIME	DISTANCE	REMARKS

		Carried Forward
		Grand Total

Total Number of Flights _____

DESTINATION:

DATE	AIRLINE	FLT. NO	AIRCRAFT TYPE	REGISTRATION	FROM	TO

JOURNAL

YEAR:

FLYING TIME	DISTANCE	REMARKS

		Carried Forward
		Grand Total

Total Number of Flights _____

DESTINATION:

DATE	AIRLINE	FLT. NO	AIRCRAFT TYPE	REGISTRATION	FROM	TO

JOURNAL

YEAR:

FLYING TIME	DISTANCE	REMARKS

Carried Forward

Grand Total

Total Number of Flights _____

DESTINATION:

DATE	AIRLINE	FLT. NO	AIRCRAFT TYPE	REGISTRATION	FROM	TO

JOURNAL

YEAR:

FLYING TIME	DISTANCE	REMARKS

Carried Forward

Grand Total

Total Number of Flights _____

DESTINATION:

DATE	AIRLINE	FLT. NO	AIRCRAFT TYPE	REGISTRATION	FROM	TO

JOURNAL

YEAR:

FLYING TIME	DISTANCE	REMARKS

		Carried Forward
		Grand Total

Total Number of Flights _____

DESTINATION:

DATE	AIRLINE	FLT. NO	AIRCRAFT TYPE	REGISTRATION	FROM	TO

JOURNAL

YEAR:

FLYING TIME	DISTANCE	REMARKS

		Carried Forward
		Grand Total

Total Number of Flights _____

DESTINATION:

DATE	AIRLINE	FLT. NO	AIRCRAFT TYPE	REGISTRATION	FROM	TO

JOURNAL

YEAR:

FLYING TIME	DISTANCE	REMARKS

Carried Forward

Grand Total

Total Number of Flights _____

DESTINATION:

DATE	AIRLINE	FLT. NO	AIRCRAFT TYPE	REGISTRATION	FROM	TO

JOURNAL

FLYING TIME	DISTANCE	REMARKS

		Carried Forward
		Grand Total

Total Number of Flights _____

DESTINATION:

DATE	AIRLINE	FLT. NO	AIRCRAFT TYPE	REGISTRATION	FROM	TO

JOURNAL

FLYING TIME	DISTANCE	REMARKS

Carried Forward

Grand Total

Total Number of Flights _____

DESTINATION:

DATE	AIRLINE	FLT. NO	AIRCRAFT TYPE	REGISTRATION	FROM	TO

JOURNAL

YEAR:

FLYING TIME	DISTANCE	REMARKS

		Carried Forward
		Grand Total

Total Number of Flights _____

DESTINATION:

DATE	AIRLINE	FLT. NO	AIRCRAFT TYPE	REGISTRATION	FROM	TO

JOURNAL

YEAR:

FLYING TIME	DISTANCE	REMARKS

Carried Forward

Grand Total

Total Number of Flights _____

DESTINATION:

DATE	AIRLINE	FLT. NO	AIRCRAFT TYPE	REGISTRATION	FROM	TO

JOURNAL

YEAR:

FLYING TIME	DISTANCE	REMARKS

Carried Forward

Grand Total

Total Number of Flights _____

DESTINATION:

DATE	AIRLINE	FLT. NO	AIRCRAFT TYPE	REGISTRATION	FROM	TO

JOURNAL

YEAR:

FLYING TIME	DISTANCE	REMARKS

Carried Forward

Grand Total

Total Number of Flights _____

DESTINATION:

DATE	AIRLINE	FLT. NO	AIRCRAFT TYPE	REGISTRATION	FROM	TO

JOURNAL

YEAR:

FLYING TIME	DISTANCE	REMARKS

Carried Forward

Grand Total

Total Number of Flights _____

DESTINATION:

DATE	AIRLINE	FLT. NO	AIRCRAFT TYPE	REGISTRATION	FROM	TO

JOURNAL

FLYING TIME	DISTANCE	REMARKS

Carried Forward

Grand Total

Total Number of Flights _____

DESTINATION:

DATE	AIRLINE	FLT. NO	AIRCRAFT TYPE	REGISTRATION	FROM	TO

JOURNAL

YEAR:

FLYING TIME	DISTANCE	REMARKS

		Carried Forward
		Grand Total

Total Number of Flights _____

DESTINATION:

DATE	AIRLINE	FLT. NO	AIRCRAFT TYPE	REGISTRATION	FROM	TO

JOURNAL

YEAR:

FLYING TIME	DISTANCE	REMARKS

Carried Forward

Grand Total

Total Number of Flights _____

DESTINATION:

DATE	AIRLINE	FLT. NO	AIRCRAFT TYPE	REGISTRATION	FROM	TO

JOURNAL

YEAR:

FLYING TIME	DISTANCE	REMARKS

Carried Forward

Grand Total

Total Number of Flights _____

DESTINATION:

DATE	AIRLINE	FLT. NO	AIRCRAFT TYPE	REGISTRATION	FROM	TO

JOURNAL

YEAR:

FLYING TIME	DISTANCE	REMARKS

Carried Forward

Grand Total

Total Number of Flights _____

DESTINATION:

DATE	AIRLINE	FLT. NO	AIRCRAFT TYPE	REGISTRATION	FROM	TO

JOURNAL

YEAR:

FLYING TIME	DISTANCE	REMARKS

Carried Forward

Grand Total

Total Number of Flights _____

DESTINATION:

DATE	AIRLINE	FLT. NO	AIRCRAFT TYPE	REGISTRATION	FROM	TO

JOURNAL

YEAR:

FLYING TIME	DISTANCE	REMARKS

Carried Forward

Grand Total

Total Number of Flights _____

DESTINATION:

DATE	AIRLINE	FLT. NO	AIRCRAFT TYPE	REGISTRATION	FROM	TO

JOURNAL

YEAR:

FLYING TIME	DISTANCE	REMARKS

Carried Forward

Grand Total

Total Number of Flights _____

DESTINATION:

DATE	AIRLINE	FLT. NO	AIRCRAFT TYPE	REGISTRATION	FROM	TO

JOURNAL

YEAR:

FLYING TIME	DISTANCE	REMARKS

		Carried Forward
		Grand Total

Total Number of Flights _____

DESTINATION:

DATE	AIRLINE	FLT. NO	AIRCRAFT TYPE	REGISTRATION	FROM	TO

JOURNAL

YEAR:

FLYING TIME	DISTANCE	REMARKS

Carried Forward

Grand Total

Total Number of Flights _____

DESTINATION:

DATE	AIRLINE	FLT. NO	AIRCRAFT TYPE	REGISTRATION	FROM	TO

JOURNAL

YEAR:

FLYING TIME	DISTANCE	REMARKS

Carried Forward

Grand Total

Total Number of Flights _____

DATE	AIRLINE	FLT. NO	AIRCRAFT TYPE	REGISTRATION	FROM	TO

JOURNAL

YEAR:

FLYING TIME	DISTANCE	REMARKS

		Carried Forward
		Grand Total

Total Number of Flights _____

DESTINATION:

DATE	AIRLINE	FLT. NO	AIRCRAFT TYPE	REGISTRATION	FROM	TO

JOURNAL

YEAR:

FLYING TIME	DISTANCE	REMARKS

Carried Forward

Grand Total

Total Number of Flights _____

DESTINATION:

DATE	AIRLINE	FLT. NO	AIRCRAFT TYPE	REGISTRATION	FROM	TO

JOURNAL

YEAR:

FLYING TIME	DISTANCE	REMARKS

		Carried Forward

Grand Total

Total Number of Flights _____

DESTINATION:

DATE	AIRLINE	FLT. NO	AIRCRAFT TYPE	REGISTRATION	FROM	TO

JOURNAL

YEAR:

FLYING TIME	DISTANCE	REMARKS

Carried Forward

Grand Total

Total Number of Flights _____

DATE	AIRLINE	FLT. NO	AIRCRAFT TYPE	REGISTRATION	FROM	TO

JOURNAL

YEAR:

FLYING TIME	DISTANCE	REMARKS

Carried Forward

Grand Total

Total Number of Flights _____

DESTINATION:

DATE	AIRLINE	FLT. NO	AIRCRAFT TYPE	REGISTRATION	FROM	TO

JOURNAL

YEAR:

FLYING TIME	DISTANCE	REMARKS

Carried Forward

Grand Total

Total Number of Flights _____

PHONETIC
ALPHABET

A   Alpha
B   Bravo
C   Charlie
D   Delta
E   Echo
F   Foxtrot
G   Golf
H   Hotel
I   India
J   Juliet
K   Kilo
L   Lima
M   Mike
N   November
O   Oscar
P   Papa
Q   Quebec
R   Romeo
S   Sierra
T   Tango
U   Uniform
V   Victor
W   Whiskey
X   X-ray
Y   Yankee
Z   Zulu